Business and Finance The Ultimate Guide

Ary S. Jr.

Published by Ary S. Jr, 2023.

While every precaution has been taken in the preparation of this book, the publisher assumes no responsibility for errors or omissions, or for damages resulting from the use of the information contained herein.

BUSINESS AND FINANCE THE ULTIMATE GUIDE

First edition. October 30, 2023.

ISBN: 979-8223220824

Written by Ary S. Jr..

Table of Contents

Business and Finances
The Ultimate Guide

Introduction

Welcome to the world of business and finance! This book is designed to provide you with a comprehensive overview of this essential topic. Whether you are a business student, an entrepreneur, or simply someone who wants to learn more about how the world of money works, this book is for you.

Business and finance are the two pillars on which the modern economy rests. Businesses need finance to operate, grow, and innovate. Finance professionals help businesses make sound financial decisions and achieve their financial goals.

This book will cover the following topics:

* The foundations of business, including business ownership structures, business models, and business strategies

* Financial statements, including the balance sheet, income statement, and cash flow statement

* Financial analysis techniques, such as ratio analysis, common-size analysis, and trend analysis

* Capital budgeting techniques, such as net present value (NPV) and internal rate of return (IRR)

* Financing options for businesses, including debt financing, equity financing, and hybrid financing

* Managing a business's finances, including cash flow management, working capital management, risk management, and financial planning and control

* Investing concepts, such as different types of investments, risk tolerance, and asset allocation

* Business valuation methods
* Mergers and acquisitions
* Business exit strategies

This book is designed to be accessible to readers with all levels of experience in business and finance. Each chapter begins with a brief overview of the topic at hand, followed by a more detailed discussion of the key concepts and techniques. Real-world examples are used throughout the book to illustrate how the concepts are applied in the real world.

By the end of this book, you will have a solid understanding of the key principles of business and finance. You will be able to make informed decisions about your own finances and the finances of your business.

Who should read this book?

This book is ideal for:

* Business students who are learning about the foundations of business and finance

* Entrepreneurs who are starting or growing their own businesses

* Investors who want to learn more about how to make sound investment decisions

* Anyone who wants to learn more about how the world of money works

How to use this book

This book can be read from cover to cover, or you can skip around to the chapters that are most relevant to your interests. Each chapter is self-contained, so you can read them in any order.

If you are new to business and finance, I recommend that you start by reading the first few chapters, which cover the foundations of business and financial statements. Once you have a good understanding of these topics, you can move on to the more advanced chapters, such as capital budgeting, investing, and business valuation.

I also encourage you to use the real-world examples throughout the book to think about how the concepts are applied in practice. Try to put yourself in the shoes of the people in the examples and make the same decisions that they did.

I hope that you enjoy this book and find it to be a valuable resource. The world of business and finance can be complex, but it is also fascinating and rewarding. I encourage you to continue learning about this important topic and to use your knowledge to achieve your financial goals.

Business and finance are two interrelated disciplines that are essential for the success of any organization. Business is the process of creating and delivering value to customers, while finance is the art and science of managing money.

Businesses need finance to operate, grow, and innovate. They need to raise capital, invest in assets, and manage their cash flow. Finance professionals help businesses make sound financial decisions and achieve their financial goals.

Here are some of the key topics that are covered in business and finance:

* Financial statements: Financial statements provide a snapshot of a company's financial performance and condition. They are used by investors, creditors, and other stakeholders to assess a company's financial health and make informed decisions.

* Ratio analysis: Ratio analysis is a technique used to compare financial statements and identify trends. It can be used to assess a company's profitability, liquidity, solvency, and efficiency.

* Budgeting and forecasting: Budgeting and forecasting are used to plan and track a company's financial performance. They help businesses to make informed decisions about how to allocate their resources and achieve their financial goals.

* Capital budgeting: Capital budgeting is the process of evaluating and selecting long-term investment projects. It involves weighing the costs and benefits of different projects to determine which ones are the most likely to generate a positive return on investment.

*Financial planning and control: Financial planning and control are used to ensure that a company's financial performance is aligned with its strategic goals. They involve setting financial targets, developing action plans to achieve those targets, and monitoring progress.

* Investing: Investing is the process of putting money to work in order to generate a financial return. Investors can choose from a variety of investment options, including stocks, bonds, mutual funds, and real estate.

* Business valuation: Business valuation is the process of determining the fair market value of a business. It is often used for tax purposes, mergers and acquisitions, and estate planning.

* Mergers and acquisitions: Mergers and acquisitions are the combination of two or more businesses into a single entity. They can be used to grow a business, expand into new markets, or acquire new technologies or capabilities.

* Business exit strategies: A business exit strategy is a plan for how a business owner will sell or otherwise exit their business. This can be done through a sale to a competitor, a public offering of stock, or a management buyout.

The Changing Landscape of Business and Finance in the 21st Century

The 21st century has seen dramatic changes in the landscape of business and finance. These changes have been driven by a number of factors, including technological innovation, globalization, and the rise of new economic powers.

One of the most significant changes has been the rise of the digital economy. The internet and other digital technologies have transformed the way businesses operate and compete. For example, e-commerce has enabled businesses to reach a global audience without having to open physical stores. Social media has also changed the way businesses interact with their customers.

Globalization has also had a major impact on business and finance. Businesses are now more likely to operate in multiple countries and to source their inputs and sell their outputs to customers around the world. This has created new opportunities for businesses, but it has also made them more vulnerable to global economic shocks and political instability.

The rise of new economic powers, such as China and India, has also changed the business and financial landscape. These countries are now major players in the global economy, and their businesses are increasingly competing with businesses from developed countries.

Financial institutions and enterprises now face a variety of difficulties as a result of these adjustments. To compete in a globalized market, businesses must be able to adapt to the quickly evolving technology landscape. Financial institutions must be capable of handling the risks brought on by the emergence of new economic powers and globalization.

Key trends in the changing landscape of business and finance

Some of the key trends in the changing landscape of business and finance include:

* The rise of the digital economy
* Globalization
* The rise of new economic powers
* The increasing importance of sustainability and social responsibility
* The growing popularity of cryptocurrencies and blockchain technology

Implications for businesses and financial institutions

The changing landscape of business and finance has several implications for businesses and financial institutions. Businesses need to be able to:

* Adapt to the rapidly changing technological landscape
* Compete in a globalized marketplace

* Manage the risks associated with globalization and the rise of new economic powers

* Develop new products and services that meet the needs of customers in the digital economy

* Operate in a sustainable and socially responsible manner

Financial institutions need to be able to:

* Manage the risks associated with the digital economy, globalization, and the rise of new economic powers

* Develop new financial products and services that meet the needs of businesses and consumers in the digital economy

* Support sustainable and socially responsible businesses

Businesses and financial institutions face a variety of opportunities and problems because of the shifting business and financial landscape. Companies and financial institutions will be well-positioned to prosper in the twenty-first century if they can adjust to these changes.

Who Should Read This Book?

This book is for anyone who wants to learn more about business and finance. Whether you are a student, an entrepreneur, an investor, or simply someone who wants to be more informed about the world of money, this book has something to offer you.

* Students: This book is an excellent resource for students who are majoring in business, finance, or economics. It provides a comprehensive overview of the key concepts and techniques in business and finance. Students will learn about the foundations of business, financial statements, financial analysis, capital budgeting, financing options, financial planning and control, investing, business valuation, mergers and acquisitions, and business exit strategies.

* Entrepreneurs: This book is also essential reading for entrepreneurs. It provides the knowledge and skills that entrepreneurs need to start and grow their businesses. Entrepreneurs will learn how to develop a business plan, secure financing, manage their finances, and make sound financial decisions.

* Investors: This book is also a valuable resource for investors. It provides the knowledge and skills that investors need to make informed investment decisions. Investors will learn about different types of investments, risk tolerance, asset allocation, and portfolio management.

* Individuals: This book is also for anyone who wants to be more informed about the world of money. It provides a basic understanding of how business and finance work. Individuals will learn about the different components of financial statements, how to read and interpret financial statements, how to budget and forecast their finances, and how to invest their money wisely.

No matter who you are or what your goals are, this book can help you learn more about business and finance. It is a comprehensive and informative resource that is suitable for readers of all levels of experience.

Chapter 1
The Foundations of Business

What Is a Business

A business is an organization that engages in the production or sale of goods or services. Businesses can be small or large, and they can operate in any industry. The goal of a business is to make a profit, which means that it must generate more revenue than it spends on expenses.

There are many different types of businesses, but they all share some common characteristics. First, businesses are typically organized as legal entities, such as sole proprietorships, partnerships, corporations, or limited liability companies (LLCs). This gives them the legal status to enter into contracts, own property, and sue and be sued.

Second, businesses typically have a specific business model. A business model describes how a business will generate revenue and profit. For example, a business might generate revenue by selling goods or services, or by advertising to consumers.

Third, businesses typically have a management team. The management team is responsible for making decisions about the business, such as what products or services to offer, where to operate, and how to market and sell the business's products or services.

Finally, businesses typically have a workforce. The workforce consists of the employees who produce or sell the business's goods or services.

Why are businesses important?

There are several reasons why businesses are significant. First, companies generate employment. Hiring new staff is necessary when a company grows or opens a new location. This stimulates the economy and lowers unemployment.

Businesses produce goods and services that people need and want. Businesses also help to innovate and develop new products and services. This helps to improve the quality of life for consumers.

Businesses generate tax revenue. Governments use tax revenue to fund important public services, such as education, healthcare, and infrastructure.

The different types of businesses

There are many different types of businesses, but they can be broadly classified into two categories: service businesses and product businesses.

Service businesses provide services to customers. Examples of service businesses include restaurants, hotels, law firms, and accounting firms.

Product businesses produce and sell goods to customers. Examples of product businesses include manufacturing companies, retail stores, and e-commerce businesses.

Businesses can also be classified according to their size.

Small businesses typically have fewer than 50 employees.

Medium-sized businesses typically have between 50 and 250 employees.

Large businesses typically have more than 250 employees.

Businesses are an important part of the economy. They create jobs, produce goods and services, and generate tax revenue. Businesses come in all shapes and sizes, and they operate in a wide variety of industries.

If you are interested in learning more about business, there are many resources available. You can take business courses at a local college or university, or you can read books and articles about business. You can also talk to entrepreneurs and business leaders to learn about their experiences.

There are many different types of businesses, but they can be broadly classified into two categories: service businesses and product businesses.

Service businesses provide services to customers. Examples of service businesses include:
* Restaurants
* Hotels
* Law firms
* Accounting firms
* Consulting firms
* IT services companies
* Financial services companies
* Healthcare providers
* Educational institutions
* Transportation companies
* Media and entertainment companies
* Telecommunications companies

Product businesses produce and sell goods to customers. Examples of product businesses include:
* Manufacturing companies
* Retail stores
* E-commerce businesses
* Agriculture and forestry businesses
* Mining and energy businesses
* Construction companies
* Real estate development companies
* Consumer goods companies
* Industrial goods companies
* Technology companies

Businesses can also be classified according to their industry. For example, businesses can be in the following industries:
* Healthcare industry
* Financial services industry
* Technology industry
* Retail industry

* Manufacturing industry
* Construction industry
* Transportation and logistics industry
* Media and entertainment industry
* Hospitality industry
* Education industry
* Government and non-profit sector

The benefits of owning a business

There are many benefits to owning a business, including:

* The ability to be your own boss
* The potential to earn a high income
* The satisfaction of creating something new and successful
* The opportunity to make a difference in the world

The challenges of owning a business

Owning a business is also challenging. Some of the challenges include:

* The need to work long hours
* The risk of financial failure
* The need to deal with a variety of problems and challenges on a daily basis

Choosing the right type of business

If you are interested in starting your own business, it is important to choose the right type of business for you. Consider your skills, interests, and experience. You should also consider the market for the products or services that you want to offer.

Once you have chosen a type of business, you need to develop a business plan. A business plan is a document that outlines your business goals and how you plan to achieve them.

Business Ownership Structures

The business ownership structure is the legal framework that determines how a business is owned and operated. There are four main types of business ownership structures: sole proprietorship, partnership, limited liability company (LLC), and corporation.

Sole proprietorship

A sole proprietorship is the simplest type of business ownership structure. It is owned and operated by one person. Sole proprietors have complete control over their businesses, but they also have unlimited personal liability. This means that they are personally responsible for all the business's debts and liabilities.

Partnership

A partnership is a business owned and operated by two or more people. Partners share in the profits and losses of the business. There are two main types of partnerships: general partnerships and limited partnerships.

In a general partnership, all partners have unlimited personal liability. In a limited partnership, there are two types of partners: general partners and limited partners. General partners have unlimited personal liability, while limited partners have limited personal liability, up to the amount of money that they have invested in the partnership.

Limited liability company (LLC)

An LLC is a hybrid business ownership structure that combines the benefits of a sole proprietorship and a corporation. LLCs offer limited personal liability to their owners, but they are not taxed as separate entities. This means that the profits and losses of the LLC pass through to the owners' personal tax returns.

Corporation

A corporation is a separate legal entity from its owners. This means that the corporation can own property, sue and be sued, and enter into contracts in its own name. Corporations offer limited personal liability to their owners, but they are taxed as separate entities. This means that the corporation pays taxes on its profits, and then the owners pay taxes on the dividends that they receive from the corporation.

Choosing the right business ownership structure

The best business ownership structure for you will depend on your individual circumstances and goals. Consider the following factors when choosing a business ownership structure:

* Personal liability: How much personal liability are you willing to accept? Sole proprietors and general partners have unlimited personal liability, while LLCs and corporations offer limited personal liability.

* Taxes: How do you want to be taxed? Sole proprietors and partnerships are pass-through entities, which means that the profits and losses of the business pass through to the owners' personal tax returns. Corporations are taxed as separate entities.

* Control: How much control do you want over your business? Sole proprietors have complete control over their businesses, while partners and shareholders in LLCs and corporations share control of the business.

* Complexity and cost: Setting up and maintaining a corporation is more complex and expensive than setting up and maintaining a sole proprietorship, partnership, or LLC.

The business ownership structure is an important decision that can have a significant impact on your business. It is important to choose the right business ownership structure for your individual circumstances and goals.

If you are unsure which business ownership structure is right for you, it is a good idea to consult with an attorney or accountant. They can help you to assess your needs and choose the best business ownership structure for your business.

Business Models

A business model is a plan for how a business will generate revenue and profit. It describes the products or services that the business will offer, the target market, the pricing strategy, and the cost structure.

There are many different types of business models, but they can be broadly classified into four categories:

* Product business models: These business models rely on the sale of products to generate revenue. Examples of product business models include:

* Retail business models: These business models involve selling products directly to consumers through physical stores or online stores.

* Manufacturing business models: These business models involve producing and selling products to other businesses or to consumers.

* Service business models: These business models rely on the provision of services to generate revenue. Examples of service business models include:

* Professional services business models: These business models involve providing professional services to clients, such as legal services, accounting services, or consulting services.

* Consumer services business models: These business models involve providing services to consumers, such as transportation services, hospitality services, or media and entertainment services.

* Subscription business models: These business models rely on recurring revenue from subscriptions. Examples of subscription business models include:

* SaaS business models: Software as a service (SaaS) business models involve providing software to customers on a subscription basis.

* Streaming business models: Streaming business models involve providing access to content, such as movies, TV shows, or music, to customers on a subscription basis.

* Marketplace business models: These business models rely on commissions or fees from transactions between buyers and sellers on the marketplace. Examples of marketplace business models include:

* E-commerce marketplace business models: These business models involve providing a platform for buyers and sellers to trade goods and services online.

* Freelancing marketplace business models: These business models involve providing a platform for businesses to hire freelancers for short-term projects.

Choosing the right business model

The best business model for you will depend on your individual circumstances and goals. Consider the following factors when choosing a business model:

* Products or services: What products or services do you want to offer?

* Target market: Who are your target customers?

* Pricing strategy: How will you price your products or services?

* Cost structure: What are your costs?

* Competitive landscape: What are the competitive forces in your industry?

The business model is an important part of any business plan. It is important to choose a business model that is aligned with your products or services, target market, pricing strategy, and cost structure.

If you are unsure which business model is right for you, it is a good idea to consult with a business advisor or mentor. They can help you to assess your needs and choose the best business model for your business.

Business Strategies

A business strategy is a plan for how a business will achieve its goals. It describes the business's long-term vision and how it plans to get there.

There are many different types of business strategies, but they can be broadly classified into three categories:

* Cost leadership strategy: A cost leadership strategy focuses on being the lowest-cost producer in the industry. This can be achieved by economies of scale, efficient production processes, and low-cost labor.

* Differentiation strategy: A differentiation strategy focuses on offering products or services that are unique and valuable to customers. This can be achieved through innovation, branding, and customer service.

* Focus strategy: A focus strategy focuses on a specific niche market or customer segment. This allows the business to tailor its products or services to the needs of its target market and to develop a deep understanding of its customers.

Choosing the right business strategy*

The best business strategy for you will depend on your industry, your competitive landscape, and your resources. Consider the following factors when choosing a business strategy:

* Industry: What are the key trends in your industry? What are the competitive forces in your industry?

* Competitive landscape: Who are your main competitors? What are their strengths and weaknesses?

* Resources: What resources do you have at your disposal? What are your strengths and weaknesses?

The business strategy is an important part of any business plan. It is important to choose a business strategy that is aligned with your industry, your competitive landscape, and your resources.

Here are some examples of successful business strategies:

* Cost leadership: A prime example of a business using this tactic is Walmart. Walmart runs on extremely low margins and has an extremely efficient supply chain, which allows them to provide lower pricing to its customers.

* Differentiation: Apple is a classic example of a company that uses a differentiation strategy. Apple products are known for their design, innovation, and user-friendly experience. Apple customers are willing to pay a premium for Apple products because they believe that they are getting a superior product.

* Focus: Tesla is a classic example of a company that uses a focus strategy. Tesla focuses on the electric vehicle market. This allows Tesla to tailor its products and services to the needs of its target market and to develop a deep understanding of its customers.

Chapter 2
Financial Statements

The Balance Sheet

The balance sheet is one of the three core financial statements, along with the income statement and the cash flow statement. It provides a snapshot of a company's financial condition at a specific point in time. The balance sheet shows the company's assets, liabilities, and equity.

Assets

Assets are everything that the company owns. They can be classified into two categories: current assets and non-current assets.

* Current assets are assets that can be converted into cash within one year. They include cash, accounts receivable, inventory, and prepaid expenses.

* Non-current assets are assets that cannot be converted into cash within one year. They include property, plant, and equipment; intangible assets; and investments.

Liabilities

Liabilities are everything that the company owes. They can be classified into two categories: current liabilities and non-current liabilities.

* Current liabilities are liabilities that must be paid within one year. They include accounts payable, accrued expenses, and short-term debt.

* Non-current liabilities are liabilities that do not have to be paid within one year. They include long-term debt and deferred taxes.

Equity

Equity is the difference between a company's assets and liabilities. It represents the ownership interest in the company.

Balance sheet equation

The balance sheet equation is as follows:

Assets = Liabilities + Equity

This equation states that the total value of a company's assets must equal the total value of its liabilities and equity.

How to read a balance sheet

When reading a balance sheet, it is important to look at the following:

* Total assets: This number shows the total value of the company's assets.

* Total liabilities: This number shows the total value of the company's liabilities.

* Total equity: This number shows the total value of the company's equity.

* Asset composition: This shows the breakdown of the company's assets by type of asset.

* Liability composition: This shows the breakdown of the company's liabilities by type of liability.

* Financial ratios: Financial ratios can be used to assess the company's financial health and performance. Some common financial ratios include the current ratio, quick ratio, debt-to-equity ratio, and return on equity.

The balance sheet is an important financial statement that can be used to assess a company's financial condition. By understanding the balance sheet and how to read it, investors and creditors can make more informed decisions about whether to invest in or lend money to a company.

The Income Statement

The income statement, also known as the profit and loss statement or P&L, is one of the three core financial statements that businesses use to report their financial performance. It shows how much revenue a business has generated and how much it has spent over a specific period, typically a quarter or a year. The income statement is used by investors, creditors, and other stakeholders to assess a business's profitability and financial health.

The income statement equation

The income statement equation is as follows:

Revenue - Expenses = Net income

This equation states that a business's net income is equal to its revenue minus its expenses. Revenue is the money that a business generates from selling its products or services. Expenses are the costs that a business incurs to generate revenue.

The different types of expenses

Expenses can be classified into two categories: operating expenses and non-operating expenses.

* Operating expenses are the costs that a business incurs in its day-to-day operations. They include things like cost of goods sold, selling and marketing expenses, and general and administrative expenses.

* Non-operating expenses are costs that are not related to a business's day-to-day operations. They may include things like interest expense and income tax expense.

How to read an income statement

When reading an income statement, it is important to look at the following:

* Revenue: This number shows the total amount of revenue that the business generated during the period.

* Gross profit: This number shows the business's gross profit, which is calculated by subtracting the cost of goods sold from revenue.

* Operating profit: This number shows the business's operating profit, which is calculated by subtracting operating expenses from gross profit.

* Net income: This number shows the business's net income, which is calculated by subtracting non-operating expenses from operating profit.

*Financial ratios

Financial ratios can be used to assess a business's profitability and financial health. Some common financial ratios that are calculated using the income statement include:

* Profit margin: This ratio measures how much profit a business generates from each dollar of revenue.

* Return on equity (ROE): This ratio measures how much profit a business generates for its shareholders.

* Return on assets (ROA): This ratio measures how efficiently a business is using its assets to generate profit.

The Cash Flow Statement

Along with the income statement and balance sheet, the cash flow statement is one of the three fundamental financial statements. It provides information on the amount of cash generated and spent by a business over a given time frame, usually a quarter or a year. Creditors, investors, and other stakeholders use the cash flow statement to evaluate a company's financial standing and capacity to pay its debts.

The different types of cash flows

Cash flows can be classified into three categories: operating cash flows, investing cash flows, and financing cash flows.

* Operating cash flows are cash flows that are generated from the company's core business activities. They include things like cash received from customers, cash paid to suppliers, and cash paid for salaries and wages.

* Investing cash flows are cash flows that are associated with the purchase and sale of long-term assets, such as property, plant, and equipment. They also include cash flows from investments in other companies.

* Financing cash flows are cash flows that are associated with the raising and repayment of debt and equity. They include things like cash received from the sale of new shares of stock, cash paid to repay debt, and cash paid to shareholders in dividends.

The cash flow statement equation

The cash flow statement equation is as follows:

Net income + non-cash expenses + Deferred taxes = Cash flow from operating activities

Cash flow from operating activities - Investing cash flows - Financing cash flows = Net change in cash and cash equivalents

This equation shows that the net change in a company's cash and cash equivalents is equal to its cash flow from operating activities minus its investing cash flows and financing cash flows.

How to read a cash flow statement

When reading a cash flow statement, it is important to look at the following:

* Net cash flow from operating activities: This number shows how much cash the company generated from its core business activities during the period.

* Net cash flow from investing activities: This number shows how much cash the company generated from the purchase and sale of long-term assets and investments during the period.

* Net cash flow from financing activities: This number shows how much cash the company generated from the raising and repayment of debt and equity during the period.

* Net change in cash and cash equivalents: This number shows the overall change in the company's cash and cash equivalents during the period.

Financial ratios

Financial ratios can be used to assess a company's liquidity and financial health. Some common financial ratios that are calculated using the cash flow statement include:

* Cash flow to debt ratio: This ratio measures a company's ability to repay its debt using its cash flow from operating activities.

* Cash flow margin: This ratio measures how much cash a company generates from each dollar of revenue.

* Free cash flow: This ratio measures the amount of cash that a company has available after it has paid its operating expenses and capital expenditures.

To read and understand financial statements, you need to have a basic understanding of accounting principles. However, even if you don't have a background in accounting, you can still learn how to read and understand financial statements by following these steps:

1. Identify the three main financial statements. The three main financial statements are the balance sheet, the income statement, and the cash flow statement. Each statement provides a different perspective on a company's financial health.

2. Understand the basic concepts of each financial statement.

* Balance sheet: The balance sheet shows a company's assets, liabilities, and equity at a specific point in time. Assets are anything that the company owns, liabilities are anything that the company owes, and equity is the difference between assets and liabilities.

* Income statement: The income statement provides information on a company's earnings over a certain time frame, usually a quarter or a year. The difference between revenue and expenses is known as net income.

* Cash flow statement: The cash flow statement displays the incoming and outgoing cash flows for a business over time. The difference between cash inflows and withdrawals is known as net cash flow.

3. Analyze the financial statements. Once you understand the basic concepts of each financial statement, you can begin to analyze them. Look for trends and patterns in the data. For example, you might look at how revenue and expenses have changed over time, or how cash flow has changed from one quarter to the next.

4. Compare the financial statements to other companies. You can also compare a company's financial statements to other companies in the

same industry. This can help you to see how the company is performing relative to its peers.

5. Use financial ratios to assess the company's financial health. Financial ratios can be used to assess a company's profitability, liquidity, and financial leverage. Some common financial ratios include the profit margin, return on equity, and debt-to-equity ratio.

Here are some additional tips for reading and understanding financial statements:

* Pay attention to the footnotes. The footnotes to the financial statements contain important information about the company's accounting policies and financial condition.

* Look for red flags. Red flags are things that could indicate that the company is in financial trouble. Some examples of red flags include declining revenue, increasing expenses, and a high debt-to-equity ratio.

* Be skeptical. Don't take everything you read in the financial statements at face value. Remember that the financial statements are prepared by the company's management, and they may have an incentive to present the company in a positive light.

Chapter 3
Financial Analysis

Ratio analysis is a technique used to assess a company's financial performance and position by comparing different financial ratios. Financial ratios are calculated using data from a company's financial statements, such as the balance sheet, income statement, and cash flow statement.

Ratio analysis can be used to:

* Assess a company's profitability. Profitability ratios measure how well a company is generating profits. Some common profitability ratios include the profit margin, return on equity (ROE), and return on assets (ROA).

* Assess a company's liquidity. Liquidity ratios measure how well a company can meet its short-term financial obligations. Some common liquidity ratios include the current ratio and quick ratio.

* Assess a company's financial leverage. Leverage ratios measure how much debt a company uses to finance its operations. Some common leverage ratios include the debt-to-equity ratio and debt-to-assets ratio.

* Compare a company's performance to other companies in the same industry. This can help to identify companies that are outperforming or underperforming their peers.

How to use ratio analysis

To use ratio analysis, you first need to identify the ratios that you want to calculate. There are many different financial ratios available, so it is important to choose the ratios that are most relevant to your analysis.

Once you have identified the ratios that you want to calculate, you can use the data from a company's financial statements to calculate the ratios.

Once you have calculated the ratios, you can compare them to industry averages and to the company's own historical performance. This can help you to identify trends and patterns in the company's financial performance.

Limitations of ratio analysis

Ratio analysis is a useful tool for assessing a company's financial performance and position, but it is important to remember that it has some limitations. First, ratios are only as good as the data that is used to calculate them. If the company's financial statements are inaccurate, the ratios will also be inaccurate.

Second, ratios should not be used in isolation. It is important to consider the company's overall financial condition and its industry environment when interpreting ratios.

Ratio analysis is a valuable tool for investors, creditors, and other stakeholders who want to assess a company's financial performance and position. By understanding the different financial ratios and how to use them, you can make more informed decisions about whether to invest in or lend money to a company.

Common size analysis is a technique used to analyze a company's financial statements by expressing each line item as a percentage of a base figure. This allows for easy comparison of financial statements over time and between companies.

The base figure used in common size analysis can vary depending on the type of financial statement being analyzed. For example, the balance sheet is typically expressed as a percentage of total assets, while the income statement is typically expressed as a percentage of revenue.

How to perform common size analysis

To perform common size analysis, simply divide each line item on the financial statement by the base figure and multiply by 100 to get a percentage. For example, to calculate the cost of goods sold as a percentage of revenue, you would divide the cost of goods sold by revenue and multiply by 100.

Benefits of common size analysis

Several advantages of common size analysis include:

* Easy comparison of financial statements over time: Common size analysis allows you to easily compare a company's financial statements over time to see how its financial performance has changed. For example, you can compare a company's gross profit margin from one year to the next to see if it has increased or decreased.

* Easy comparison of financial statements between companies: Common size analysis also allows you to easily compare the financial statements of different companies in the same industry to see how they perform relative to each other. For example, you can compare the net profit margin of two different retail companies to see which company is more profitable.

* Identification of trends and patterns: Common size analysis can help you to identify trends and patterns in a company's financial performance. For example, you can look for trends in a company's gross profit margin, operating profit margin, and net profit margin to see how its profitability has changed over time.

Limitations of common size analysis

Common size analysis is a useful tool, but it is important to remember that it has some limitations. First, common size analysis does not take into account the size of a company. As a result, it is not possible to compare the financial statements of two companies of different sizes directly.

Common size analysis can be distorted by accounting changes. For example, if a company changes its accounting method for inventory valuation, this can impact its cost of goods sold and gross profit margin.

Common size analysis is a valuable tool for investors, creditors, and other stakeholders who want to analyze a company's financial performance over time and compare it to other companies in the same industry.

Businesses utilize forecasting and budgeting as two fundamental financial management tools to plan and control their spending. Forecasting is the process of projecting a company's future financial performance, whereas budgeting is planning for how a corporation will use its resources over a given period of time.

Why are budgeting and forecasting important?

Budgeting and forecasting help businesses to track their progress and identify potential problems early on. By comparing their actual financial performance to their budget and forecast, businesses can identify areas where they are overspending or where they may need to adjust their plans.

Budgeting and forecasting help businesses to make better decisions about how to allocate their resources. By understanding their financial needs and priorities, businesses can make sure that they are spending their money in the most efficient and effective way possible.

How to create a budget

Although there are many variations on how to make a budget, the fundamental procedures remain the same:

1. Identify your income sources. This includes all of the ways that your business generates revenue, such as sales, fees, and investments.

2. Estimate your expenses. This includes all of the costs that your business incurs, such as rent, salaries, and marketing costs.

3. Categorize your expenses. This will help you to track where your money is going. Common expense categories include operating expenses, marketing expenses, and capital expenditures.

4. Set spending limits for each expense category. This is where you decide how much money you are willing to spend on each category.

5. Track your actual spending and compare it to your budget. This will help you to identify areas where you are overspending or where you may need to adjust your plans.

How to create a forecast

The technique of projecting future financial performance for a corporation is called forecasting. Although there are many distinct forecasting techniques, the following are the most widely used ones:

* Time series forecasting: This method uses historical data to predict future performance.

* Causal forecasting: This method uses cause-and-effect relationships to predict future performance.

* Judgmental forecasting: This method uses expert judgment to predict future performance.

How to use budgeting and forecasting together

Budgeting and forecasting are two complementary tools that can be used together to improve a business's financial management. By using budgeting to set spending limits and forecasting to predict future financial performance, businesses can make more informed decisions about how to allocate their resources and achieve their goals.

Here are some examples of how budgeting and forecasting can be used together:

* A company's budget can be used to establish expenditure caps for marketing costs. The company can then utilize forecasting to estimate the volume of leads and sales that the marketing initiatives will produce. Subsequently, this data can be employed to assess the marketing campaigns' efficacy and modify the budget accordingly.

* A business can use its budget to set spending limits for capital expenditures. Then, the business can use forecasting to predict the future demand for its products or services. This information can then be used to determine which capital expenditures are necessary and when they should be made.

* A business can use its budget to set spending limits for research and development expenses. Then, the business can use forecasting to predict the potential revenue from new products or services. This information

can then be used to evaluate the return on investment of research and development projects.

Chapter 4
Capital Budgeting

What is capital budgeting?

Capital budgeting is the process of evaluating long-term investments to determine which ones are worth making. It is a systematic approach to analyzing and comparing different investment options. Capital budgeting decisions are typically made by businesses, but individuals and governments can also use capital budgeting to evaluate investment opportunities.

Why is capital budgeting important?

Because it enables organizations to make well-informed investment decisions, capital budgeting is crucial. Prior to selecting a choice, it is crucial to thoroughly consider all the available possibilities because capital expenditures can be costly and dangerous. Businesses that use capital budgeting can:

* Identify the most profitable investment opportunities
* Reduce the risk of making bad investments
* Allocate resources efficiently
* Improve financial performance

How to do capital budgeting

While there are many distinct approaches to capital budgeting, the following are the most widely used ones:

* Net present value (NPV): NPV calculates the present value of all future cash flows from an investment. A positive NPV indicates that the

investment is expected to generate a return that is greater than the cost of capital.

* Internal rate of return (IRR): IRR is the discount rate that makes the NPV of an investment equal to zero. A higher IRR indicates that an investment is more profitable.

* Payback period: Payback period calculates the amount of time it takes for an investment to generate enough cash flows to cover its initial cost. A shorter payback period indicates that an investment is less risky.

Which capital budgeting method should I use?

Many variables, including the nature of the investment, the investor's risk tolerance, and the information's accessibility, determine the optimal capital budgeting technique to employ.

* NPV is the most comprehensive capital budgeting method, but it requires the most information to calculate. It is a good choice for evaluating complex investments with long payback periods.

* RR is easier to calculate than NPV, but it can be misleading if the investment has multiple cash flows or if the cash flows are not evenly distributed over time. It is a good choice for evaluating investments with short payback periods.

* Despite not accounting for time worth of money, the payback period is the most basic capital budgeting technique. For assessing high-risk ventures, it is a good option.

Businesses can employ a variety of capital budgeting strategies to assess long-term investments and choose which ones are worthwhile. The following are a few of the most popular capital budgeting strategies:

*Net present value (NPV): This discounting method determines the present value of all future cash flows from an investment by using the net present value formula. When an investment has a positive net present value (NPV), it means that the expected return will exceed the cost of capital. Although net present value (NPV) is regarded as the most thorough capital budgeting method, its computation can be challenging and needs precise projections of future cash flows.

* Internal rate of return (IRR): IRR is another discounting technique that calculates the discount rate that makes the NPV of an investment equal to zero. A higher IRR indicates that an investment is more profitable. IRR is relatively easy to calculate, but it can be misleading if the investment has multiple cash flows or if the cash flows are not evenly distributed over time.

* Payback period: This basic capital budgeting method determines how long it will take an investment to produce sufficient cash flows to cover its initial cost. Investments with shorter payback periods are often considered to be less hazardous. The payback period is a useful metric for evaluating possible investments, but it ignores cash flows that are created beyond the payback period and the time value of money.

* Profitability index (PI): PI is a capital budgeting technique that is calculated by dividing the NPV of an investment by its initial cost. A PI greater than 1 indicates that the investment is expected to generate a return that is greater than the cost of capital. PI is a good tool for comparing different investment options, but it is important to note that it is based on the same assumptions as NPV.

* Modified internal rate of return (MIRR): MIRR is a capital planning method that is comparable to IRR but accounts for the cash flow reinvestment rate. MIRR is a useful metric for assessing investments that have varying rates of return on investment, like capital expenditures for new machinery or product development.

How to choose the right capital budgeting technique

A multitude of considerations, including the nature of the investment, the investor's risk tolerance, and the accessibility of information, determine which capital budgeting technique is most appropriate.

* NPV is a good choice for evaluating complex investments with long payback periods, such as investments in new plant and equipment.

* IRR is a good choice for evaluating investments with short payback periods, such as investments in new marketing campaigns or working capital.

* Payback period is a good tool for screening potential investments and identifying those that are less risky.

* PI is a good tool for comparing different investment options and identifying those that are expected to generate a return that is greater than the cost of capital.

* MIRR is a good tool for evaluating investments with different reinvestment rates.

It is important to note that no single capital budgeting technique is perfect. Each technique has its own advantages and disadvantages. Therefore, it is important to use multiple capital budgeting techniques and to consider other factors, such as the strategic goals of the business and the risk tolerance of the investor, when making investment decisions.

How to make sound capital budgeting decisions

Capital budgeting decisions are some of the most important decisions that businesses make. These decisions can have a significant impact on a company's financial performance and long-term success. Therefore, it is important to make sound capital budgeting decisions.

Here are some tips for making sound capital budgeting decisions:

1. Identify and evaluate all of the potential investment options. This includes both internal and external investment opportunities.

2. Gather accurate and reliable information about each investment option. This includes information about the investment's costs, benefits, and risks.

3. Use multiple capital budgeting techniques to evaluate the investment options. This will help you to get a more complete picture of the potential risks and rewards of each investment.

4. Consider the strategic goals of the business when making investment decisions. This will help you to identify investments that are aligned with the company's overall strategy.

5. Consider the risk tolerance of the business when making investment decisions. This will help you to avoid making investments that are too risky for the company.

6. Get input from other stakeholders before making investment decisions. This could include other members of management, the board of directors, or financial advisors.

Here are some additional tips for making sound capital budgeting decisions:

* Use realistic assumptions. When evaluating investment options, it is important to use realistic assumptions about future costs, benefits, and risks. Overly optimistic assumptions can lead to bad investment decisions.

* Be aware of the biases that can affect your decision-making. There are a number of cognitive biases that can affect the way that we make decisions. It is important to be aware of these biases so that you can avoid making irrational decisions.

* Don't be afraid to say no. Not all investment opportunities are created equal. It is important to be able to say no to investment opportunities that are not a good fit for your business.

Chapter 5

Financing Your Business

Debt financing is a type of financing in which a business borrows money from a lender and agrees to repay the loan with interest over a period of time. Debt financing is one of the most common forms of financing for businesses of all sizes.

Advantages of debt financing

The use of debt finance has several benefits, such as:

* No ownership dilution: To borrow money, businesses are not required to give up any equity in their projects. On the other hand, equity financing entails a business selling ownership shares to generate capital.

* Tax benefits: Interest payments on debt are typically tax-deductible, which can reduce the overall cost of the debt financing.

* Flexibility: Debt financing can be used for a variety of purposes, such as financing growth, expanding operations, or acquiring other businesses.

Disadvantages of debt financing

There are also some disadvantages to using debt financing, including:

* Repayment obligations: Businesses that use debt financing have a legal obligation to repay the loan with interest. This can put a strain on the company's cash flow, especially if the business is not generating enough revenue.

* Risk of default: If a business is unable to repay its debt, it may default on the loan. This can damage the company's credit rating and make it difficult to borrow money in the future.

* Financial covenants: Lenders may impose financial covenants on businesses that borrow money. Financial covenants are restrictions on the company's financial activities, such as debt-to-equity ratios and minimum cash flow requirements.

Types of debt financing

There are a number of different types of debt financing available to businesses, including:

* Bank loans: Bank loans are the most common type of debt financing. Banks offer a variety of different loan products, such as term loans, lines of credit, and commercial mortgages.

*Bonds: Bonds are essentially IOUs that businesses issue to investors. Investors who purchase bonds receive regular interest payments from the business and are repaid the principal amount of the bond when it matures.

* Commercial paper: Commercial paper is a short-term debt security that businesses use to finance their working capital needs. Commercial paper is typically repaid within 90 days.

* Invoice financing: Invoice financing is a type of debt financing in which a business borrows money against its outstanding invoices. This type of financing can be helpful for businesses that have long payment terms.

How to choose the right type of debt financing

The best type of debt financing for a business will depend on several factors, such as the size of the business, the purpose of the financing, and the credit rating of the business. Businesses should carefully consider all their options before choosing a type of debt financing.

Equity financing is a type of financing in which a business sells shares of ownership to investors. Investors who purchase shares of equity in a business become shareholders and have a right to a portion of the company's profits and assets.

Advantages of equity financing

The use of equity financing has several benefits, such as:

* No repayment obligations: Businesses that raise capital through equity financing do not have to repay the money to the investors. This gives businesses more flexibility with their cash flow.

* No financial covenants: Investors in equity financing do not typically impose financial covenants on businesses. This gives businesses more freedom to make decisions about how to operate their businesses.

* Potential for higher returns: Equity investors have the potential to earn higher returns on their investment than debt investors. This is because equity investors are entitled to a portion of the company's profits, which can grow over time.

Disadvantages of equity financing

There are also some disadvantages to using equity financing, including:

* Dilution of ownership: When a business sells shares of equity, it is giving up a portion of ownership in the company. This can make it more difficult for the original owners to maintain control of the business.

* Cost of capital: Equity financing can be more expensive than debt financing. This is because equity investors expect to earn a higher return on their investment than debt investors.

* Less flexibility: Businesses that raise capital through equity financing may be under more pressure to perform well in the short term. This is because equity investors want to see the company grow and generate profits so that they can earn a return on their investment.

Types of equity financing

Enterprises can choose from a variety of equity financing options, such as:

* Public offerings: Public offerings are equity financings that are registered with the Securities and Exchange Commission (SEC). Public

offerings are typically used by large companies to raise capital from a wide range of investors.

* Private placements: Private placements are equity financings that are not registered with the SEC. Private placements are typically used by small and medium-sized businesses to raise capital from a limited number of accredited investors.

* Venture capital (VC): VC is a type of equity financing that is provided to early-stage companies with high growth potential. VC investors typically invest in companies that are developing new products or services or that are expanding into new markets.

* Angel investors: Angel investors are individuals who invest their own money in early-stage companies. Angel investors are typically motivated by the potential to earn high returns on their investment and by the opportunity to help entrepreneurs build successful businesses.

How to choose the right type of equity financing

A company's ideal form of equity financing will vary depending on several elements, including its size, stage of development, and sector of the market it serves. Enterprises must thoroughly evaluate all available alternatives prior to selecting a kind of equity financing.

Hybrid financing is a type of financing that combines elements of debt financing and equity financing. Hybrid financing instruments typically have characteristics of both debt and equity, such as the right to receive interest payments and the right to participate in the company's profits.

Advantages of hybrid financing

The use of hybrid financing has several benefits, such as:

* Flexibility: Hybrid financing can provide businesses with more flexibility than debt or equity financing alone. For example, some hybrid financing instruments may allow businesses to defer interest payments or to convert the debt into equity.

* Access to capital: Hybrid financing can help businesses to access capital that they might not be able to access through debt or equity

financing alone. For example, businesses with poor credit ratings may be able to qualify for hybrid financing.

* Alignment of interests: Hybrid financing can align the interests of the business and its investors. For example, hybrid financing instruments that give investors the right to participate in the company's profits can incentivize investors to help the business to grow and succeed.

Disadvantages of hybrid financing

There are also some disadvantages to using hybrid financing, including:

* Complexity: Hybrid financing instruments can be complex and difficult to understand. This can make it difficult for businesses to choose the right hybrid financing instrument for their needs and to negotiate the terms of the financing with investors.

* Cost: Hybrid financing can be more expensive than debt or equity financing alone. This is because hybrid financing instruments typically have higher interest rates than debt financing and give investors more rights than equity financing.

* Risk: Hybrid financing instruments can be riskier than debt or equity financing alone. This is because hybrid financing instruments typically have subordination clauses, which mean that investors in hybrid financing will be paid back after other creditors in the event of a bankruptcy.

Types of hybrid financing

There are several varieties of hybrid finance instruments on the market, such as:

* Convertible debt: Convertible debt is a type of debt that can be converted into equity shares at the holder's option. Convertible debt is a popular type of hybrid financing for early-stage companies and companies that are experiencing rapid growth.

* Preferred equity: Preferred equity is a type of equity that gives investors certain preferential rights, such as the right to receive fixed dividends and the right to be paid back before common equity

shareholders in the event of a bankruptcy. Preferred equity is a popular type of hybrid financing for companies that need to raise capital but want to maintain control of the business.

* Mezzanine financing: Mezzanine financing is a type of debt that has characteristics of both debt and equity. Mezzanine loans typically have higher interest rates than traditional bank loans, but they may also have features that make them more flexible, such as the right to convert the debt into equity. Mezzanine financing is a popular type of hybrid financing for middle-market companies.

How to choose the right type of hybrid financing

The best type of hybrid financing for a business will depend on a few factors, such as the size of the business, the stage of the business's development, and the industry in which the business operates. Businesses should carefully consider all their options before choosing a type of hybrid financing.

Choosing the right financing structure for your business is an important decision. It can have a significant impact on your business's growth, profitability, and overall success.

When selecting a funding structure, there are several things to take into account:

* The size of your business: Larger businesses typically have more options available to them than smaller businesses.

* The stage of your business: Early-stage businesses may have different financing needs than more established businesses.

* The industry in which you operate: Some industries are more capital-intensive than others.

* Your business's credit rating: A good credit rating can give you access to lower interest rates and more flexible financing terms.

* Your business's financial projections: Lenders and investors will want to see that your business has a realistic plan for how it will repay the financing.

Here are some tips for choosing the right financing structure for your business:

* Identify your financing needs. What is the purpose of the financing? How much money do you need to raise? Over what period of time do you need to repay the financing?

* Evaluate your options. There are a variety of financing options available, including debt financing, equity financing, and hybrid financing. Consider the advantages and disadvantages of each option and choose the one that is best suited to your business's needs.

* Get quotes from multiple lenders or investors. This will help you to compare interest rates and terms and to find the best deal for your business.

* Negotiate the terms of the financing. Don't be afraid to negotiate the terms of the financing to get the best deal possible.

Here are some examples of different financing structures:

* Debt financing: This type of financing entails taking out a loan from a lender, like a credit union or bank. Over time, interest must be paid back on debt funding.

* Equity financing: Equity financing involves selling shares of ownership in your business to investors. Equity investors expect to receive a return on their investment, which can come in the form of dividends or capital gains.

* Hybrid financing: Hybrid financing is a combination of debt and equity financing. Hybrid financing instruments typically have characteristics of both debt and equity, such as the right to receive interest payments and the right to participate in the company's profits.

If you are not sure which financing structure is right for your business, it is a good idea to consult with a financial advisor. A financial advisor can help you to assess your needs and to choose the financing option that is best suited to your business's goals.

Chapter 6
Managing Your Business's Finances

C ash flow management is the process of tracking and controlling the inflow and outflow of cash in a business. It is an important part of financial management, as it helps businesses to ensure that they have enough cash to meet their financial obligations and to take advantage of growth opportunities.

Why is cash flow management important?

The following are some reasons why cash flow management is crucial:

* Ensures that businesses have enough cash to meet their financial obligations. This includes paying suppliers, employees, and taxes.

* Helps businesses to identify and address potential cash flow problems early on. This can help to prevent businesses from running out of cash and from having to take on expensive debt.

* Enables businesses to take advantage of growth opportunities. For example, businesses may need to invest in new inventory or equipment to meet increased demand.

* Improves businesses' financial performance. Businesses with good cash flow management are typically more profitable and less risky.

How to manage cash flow

Effective cash flow management is achievable for firms through a variety of strategies, such as:

* Track cash flow. This involves creating a budget and tracking actual cash inflows and outflows. This information can then be used to identify trends and patterns in cash flow.

* Forecast cash flow. This involves predicting future cash inflows and outflows. This information can then be used to make informed decisions about financial planning and budgeting.

* Manage cash inflows. This includes accelerating the collection of receivables and delaying payments to suppliers.

* Manage cash outflows. This includes reducing expenses and negotiating better payment terms with suppliers.

Tips for improving cash flow.

Here are some tips for improving cash flow:

* Offer discounts for early payment. This can encourage customers to pay their invoices more quickly.

* Charge late payment fees. This can discourage customers from paying their invoices late.

* Negotiate better payment terms with suppliers. For example, you may be able to negotiate longer payment terms or to pay in installments.

* Reduce unnecessary expenses. Review your expenses carefully and identify any areas where you can cut back.

* Use technology to automate tasks. This can free up your time so that you can focus on more important tasks, such as managing cash flow.

Cash flow management is an important part of financial management. By effectively managing their cash flow, businesses can ensure that they have enough cash to meet their financial obligations, take advantage of growth opportunities, and improve their financial performance.

Working capital management is the process of optimizing the use of current assets and liabilities to ensure that a business has enough cash to meet its short-term financial obligations. It involves balancing the inflow and outflow of cash to ensure that the business has sufficient cash to operate efficiently and effectively.

Why is working capital management important?

Several factors make working capital management crucial, including:

* Ensures that businesses have enough cash to meet their short-term financial obligations. This includes paying suppliers, employees, and taxes.

* Helps businesses to avoid cash flow problems. Cash flow problems can lead to financial difficulties, such as late payments to suppliers and employees, and can even lead to bankruptcy.

* Improves businesses' profitability. Businesses with good working capital management are typically more profitable, as they are able to take advantage of discounts and other opportunities that require upfront cash payments.

* Reduces businesses' risk. Businesses with good working capital management are less likely to default on their debt obligations and are better able to withstand unexpected events, such as economic downturns.

How to manage working capital

Effective working capital management is possible for firms through a variety of means, such as:

* Track working capital. This involves creating a budget and tracking actual working capital metrics, such as current assets, current liabilities, and net working capital. This information can then be used to identify trends and patterns in working capital.

* Forecast working capital. This involves predicting future working capital needs. This information can then be used to make informed decisions about financial planning and budgeting.

* Manage current assets. This includes managing inventory, receivables, and cash. Businesses should strive to reduce inventory levels, accelerate the collection of receivables, and invest cash in short-term, low-risk investments.

* Manage current liabilities. This includes managing accounts payable and short-term debt. Businesses should negotiate better payment

terms with suppliers and avoid borrowing too much money on a short-term basis.

Tips for improving working capital management.

Here are some tips for improving working capital management:

* Offer discounts for early payment. This can encourage customers to pay their invoices more quickly.

* Charge late payment fees. This can discourage customers from paying their invoices late.

* Negotiate better payment terms with suppliers. For example, you may be able to negotiate longer payment terms or to pay in installments.

* Reduce inventory levels. This can free up cash that can be used for other purposes.

* Accelerate the collection of receivables. This can be done by offering discounts for early payment and by following up on late payments promptly.

* Invest cash in short-term, low-risk investments. This can generate income and help to improve cash flow.

* Avoid borrowing too much money on a short-term basis. Short-term debt can be expensive and can increase the risk of financial problems.

Working capital management is an important part of financial management. By effectively managing their working capital, businesses can ensure that they have enough cash to meet their short-term financial obligations, avoid cash flow problems, improve their profitability, and reduce their risk.

Risk management is the process of identifying, assessing, and mitigating risks. It is an important part of financial management, as it helps businesses to protect themselves from financial losses and to achieve their financial goals.

Why is risk management important?

Risk management is important for several reasons:

* Protects businesses from financial losses. Risks can arise from a variety of sources, such as changes in economic conditions, financial markets, and customer preferences. Risk management can help businesses to reduce the impact of these risks on their financial performance.

* Helps businesses to make informed decisions. By understanding the risks that they face, businesses can make more informed decisions about their investments, operations, and financing.

*Improves businesses' financial performance. Businesses with good risk management are typically more profitable and less risky.

* Increases businesses' attractiveness to investors and lenders. Investors and lenders are more likely to invest in and lend money to businesses with good risk management practices in place.

How to manage risk

The risk management process typically involves the following steps:

1. Identify risk. This involves identifying all of the potential risks that could affect the business. Risks can be internal or external. Internal risks include things like operational inefficiencies, employee fraud, and product defects. External risks include things like economic downturns, changes in government regulations, and natural disasters.

2. Assess risks. Once risks have been identified, they need to be assessed to determine their likelihood and impact. The likelihood of a risk occurring is the probability that the risk will happen. The impact of a risk is the severity of the consequences if the risk does occur.

3. Mitigate risks. Once risks have been assessed, businesses need to develop and implement strategies to mitigate the risks. Risk mitigation strategies can be used to reduce the likelihood of a risk occurring, reduce the impact of a risk if it does occur, or transfer the risk to another party.

4. Monitor and review risks. The risk management process is not a one-time event. It is important to monitor and review risks on an ongoing basis to ensure that the risk mitigation strategies are effective and that new risks are identified and assessed.

Tips for effective risk management

Here are some tips for effective risk management:

* Involve all stakeholders. Risk management should be a collaborative process that involves all stakeholders, including management, employees, and customers.

* Use a risk management framework. There are a number of different risk management frameworks available. Using a framework can help businesses to identify, assess, and mitigate risks in a systematic and organized way.

* Tailor the risk management process to the business. The risk management process should be tailored to the specific needs of the business. There is no one-size-fits-all approach to risk management.

* Monitor and review the risk management process on an ongoing basis. The risk management process should be monitored and reviewed on an ongoing basis to ensure that it is effective and that it is adapted to changes in the business environment.

Risk management is an important part of financial management. By effectively managing risk, businesses can protect themselves from financial losses, make more informed decisions, improve their financial performance, and increase their attractiveness to investors and lenders.

Financial planning and control are the process of developing and implementing financial plans to achieve organizational goals. It involves setting financial objectives, forecasting financial performance, and monitoring and controlling actual financial results.

Why is financial planning and control important?

There are several reasons why financial planning and control are crucial.

* Helps businesses to achieve their financial goals. By developing and implementing financial plans, businesses can identify the resources they need and make decisions about how to allocate those resources to achieve their goals.

* Improves businesses' financial performance. Businesses with good financial planning and control practices are typically more profitable and less risky.

* Helps businesses to avoid financial problems. By monitoring and controlling actual financial results, businesses can identify and address potential financial problems early on.

* Increases businesses' attractiveness to investors and lenders. Investors and lenders are more likely to invest in and lend money to businesses with good financial planning and control practices in place.

The financial planning processes.

The financial planning process typically involves the following steps:

1. Set financial objectives. What does the business want to achieve financially? This could include things like increasing sales, profitability, and market share.

2. Forecast financial performance. How will the business achieve its financial objectives? This involves forecasting future revenue, expenses, and cash flow.

3. Develop a financial plan. The financial plan should outline the business's financial objectives, forecasts, and strategies for achieving those objectives.

4. Implement the financial plan. This involves putting the financial plan into action and making the necessary decisions to allocate resources and achieve the business's financial objectives.

5. Monitor and control financial performance. The business should monitor and control its actual financial results to ensure that it is on track to achieve its financial objectives.

Financial planning tools and techniques

Businesses can utilize a variety of tools and methods for financial planning, such as:

* Budgeting: Budgeting is the process of creating a plan for how the business will spend its money. Budgets can be used for a variety of

purposes, such as forecasting revenue and expenses, planning for capital expenditures, and controlling cash flow.

* Forecasting: Forecasting is the process of predicting future financial performance. Businesses can use a variety of forecasting methods, such as time series analysis, causal analysis, and judgmental forecasting.

* Financial ratios: Financial ratios are used to analyze the business's financial performance. Financial ratios can be used to assess the business's profitability, liquidity, and efficiency.

* Scenario planning: Scenario planning is a process that businesses can use to identify and assess the potential impact of different future events. Scenario planning can help businesses to develop contingency plans and to make more informed decisions about their future.

Financial planning and control are an important part of financial management. By effectively managing their financial planning and control process, businesses can improve their financial performance, avoid financial problems, and increase their attractiveness to investors and lenders.

Chapter 7
Investing

D ifferent types of investments*
Investing is the process of putting money into an asset with the expectation of generating a return. There are a variety of different types of investments available, each with its own risks and rewards.

Here is an overview of some of the most common types of investments:

Stocks:

Stocks are shares of ownership in a company. When you buy stock in a company, you are essentially buying a piece of that company. Stocks can be a good way to grow your wealth over time, but they are also a relatively risky investment.

Bonds:

Bonds are loans that you can give to a business or the government. Purchasing a bond is equivalent to making a fixed-rate loan to the bond's issuer for the duration of the bond's maturity. Although they have a smaller potential return than stocks, bonds are typically thought to be a less risky investment.

Mutual funds:

Mutual funds are investment vehicles that pool money from many investors and invest it in a diversified portfolio of assets. Mutual funds can be a good way to invest in a variety of different asset classes, such as stocks, bonds, and money market instruments, without having to pick individual investments yourself.

Exchange-traded funds (ETFs)

ETFs trade on an exchange like stocks, but they are like mutual funds. ETFs have several benefits over mutual funds, including more transparency and cheaper fees.

Real estate:

Real estate can be a good way to generate income and build wealth over time. However, real estate is also a relatively illiquid investment, meaning that it can be difficult to sell quickly if you need to.

Commodities: Commodities are raw materials, such as oil, gold, and wheat. Commodities can be a good way to hedge against inflation and to diversify your investment portfolio. However, commodities are also a relatively volatile investment, meaning that their prices can fluctuate wildly.

Cash and cash equivalents: Cash and cash equivalents are the most liquid investments, meaning that they can be easily converted into cash. However, cash and cash equivalents typically offer the lowest returns of all the different types of investments.

Which type of investment is right for you?

The best type of investment for you will depend on your individual circumstances, including your financial goals, risk tolerance, and investment horizon. If you are unsure which type of investment is right for you, it is a good idea to consult with a financial advisor.

Here are some additional tips for choosing the right investments:

* Consider your financial goals. What are you saving for? Retirement? A down payment on a house? A child's education? Once you know your financial goals, you can choose investments that are aligned with those goals.

* Understand your risk tolerance. How much risk are you comfortable with? Some investments are riskier than others. If you are not comfortable with risk, you may want to choose more conservative investments.

* Diversify your portfolio. Don't put all your eggs in one basket. Spread your money across a variety of different investments to reduce your risk.

* Rebalance your portfolio regularly. As your investments grow and change, you will need to rebalance your portfolio to ensure that it remains aligned with your financial goals and risk tolerance.

Investing can be a great way to grow your wealth over time. However, it is important to understand the risks involved before you invest. By choosing the right investments and diversifying your portfolio, you can reduce your risk and increase your chances of success.

Asset allocation is the process of dividing your investment portfolio among different asset classes. The three main asset classes are equities, fixed income, and cash and cash equivalents. Equities include stocks and other investments that represent ownership in a company. Fixed income includes bonds and other investments that provide a fixed stream of income. Cash and cash equivalents include investments that can be easily converted into cash, such as money market accounts and certificates of deposit.

Why is asset allocation important?

The following are some reasons why asset allocation matters:

* It helps to reduce risk. By diversifying your portfolio across different asset classes, you can reduce your overall risk. This is because different asset classes tend to perform differently under different market conditions. For example, when the stock market is down, the bond market may be up. By investing in both stocks and bonds, you can reduce your overall risk of loss.

* It helps to achieve your financial goals. Different asset classes offer different potential returns. Equities offer the highest potential returns, but they are also the riskiest asset class. Fixed income offers lower potential returns, but it is also a less risky asset class. Cash and cash equivalents offer the lowest potential returns, but they are also the most

liquid asset class. By choosing the right asset allocation, you can balance your risk and return objectives to achieve your financial goals.

How to determine your asset allocation

The best asset allocation for you will depend on your individual circumstances, including your financial goals, risk tolerance, and investment horizon. If you are unsure how to determine your asset allocation, it is a good idea to consult with a financial advisor.

Here are some general guidelines for determining your asset allocation:

* Consider your financial goals. What are you saving for? Retirement? A down payment on a house? A child's education? The closer you are to your financial goals, the more conservative your asset allocation should be. This is because you don't have as much time to recover from any losses.

* Understand your risk tolerance. How much risk are you comfortable with? Some people are more comfortable with risk than others. If you are not comfortable with risk, you may want to choose a more conservative asset allocation.

* Choose investments that are appropriate for your investment horizon. Your investment horizon is the length of time you plan to invest your money. If you are investing for the long term, you may want to choose a more aggressive asset allocation. This is because you have more time to recover from any losses and to benefit from the potential growth of the stock market over time.

Rebalancing your portfolio

Your asset allocation is not a one-time event. As your investments grow and change, you will need to rebalance your portfolio to ensure that it remains aligned with your financial goals and risk tolerance. Rebalancing typically involves selling some of your investments that have outperformed and buying more of your investments that have underperformed. This helps to maintain your desired asset allocation and reduce your overall risk.

Asset allocation is an important part of financial planning. By choosing the right asset allocation for your individual circumstances, you can reduce your risk and increase your chances of success in achieving your financial goals.

Portfolio management is the process of selecting, monitoring, rebalancing, and adjusting a portfolio of investments to meet the investor's objectives, risk tolerance, and time horizon. It is an active process that requires the investor to regularly review their portfolio and make changes as needed.

The portfolio management process

The portfolio management process typically involves the following steps:

1. Define investment objectives. What are the investor's financial goals? What is their risk tolerance? What is their time horizon?

2. Asset allocation. The investor must decide how to allocate their assets among different asset classes, such as stocks, bonds, and cash.

3. Security selection. The investor must then select individual securities within each asset class.

4. Portfolio monitoring. The investor must regularly monitor their portfolio to ensure that it is on track to meet their investment objectives.

5. Portfolio rebalancing. The investor may need to rebalance their portfolio periodically to ensure that it remains aligned with their investment objectives and risk tolerance.

Portfolio management strategies

Investors have access to a multitude of portfolio management techniques. The following are a few popular tactics:

* Active management: Active portfolio managers attempt to outperform the market by buying and selling securities on a regular basis.

* Passive management: Passive portfolio managers invest in index funds or other investments that track a specific market index.

* Asset-based management: Asset-based portfolio managers focus on asset allocation and security selection. They typically invest in a

diversified portfolio of assets and hold their investments for the long term.

* Risk-based management: Risk-based portfolio managers focus on managing risk. They typically use a variety of risk management tools, such as stop-loss orders and hedges, to protect their portfolios from losses.

Which portfolio management strategy is right for you?

The best portfolio management strategy for you will depend on your individual circumstances, including your financial goals, risk tolerance, and investment horizon. If you are unsure which portfolio management strategy is right for you, it is a good idea to consult with a financial advisor.

Here are some additional tips for portfolio management:

* Diversify your portfolio. Don't put all your eggs in one basket. Spread your money across a variety of different investments to reduce your risk.

* Rebalance your portfolio regularly. As your investments grow and change, you will need to rebalance your portfolio to ensure that it remains aligned with your investment objectives and risk tolerance.

* Don't panic sell. When the market is down, it is important to stay calm and avoid panic selling. Remember that the market will eventually recover.

* Invest for the long term. Don't try to time the market. The best way to build wealth over time is to invest for the long term.

Chapter 8
Business Valuation

Business valuation is the process of determining the economic value of a business. It is an important part of many business transactions, such as mergers and acquisitions, buyouts, and estate planning.

Values for businesses can be determined using a variety of techniques, such as these:

* Income approach: This approach values a business based on its future earnings potential.

* Asset approach: This approach values a business based on the net value of its assets.

* Market approach: This approach values a business based on the prices of comparable businesses that have recently sold.

The best method to use for valuing a business will depend on the specific circumstances of the business. In many cases, a combination of methods will be used to get the most accurate valuation.

Why is business valuation important?

There are several reasons why business valuation is crucial.

* It helps to ensure that buyers and sellers of businesses are paying a fair price.

* It can be used to attract investors and lenders. A business with a high valuation is more likely to attract investors and lenders who are willing to provide financing.

* It can be used to make informed business decisions. For example, a business valuation can be used to decide whether to expand into a new market or to launch a new product line.

How to value a business

The process of valuing a business can be complex and time-consuming. It is important to consult with a qualified business valuation professional to get an accurate valuation.

Here are some general steps involved in the business valuation process:

1. Gather financial information. This includes information such as the business's income statement, balance sheet, and cash flow statement.

2. Analyze the business's industry and market. This includes understanding the competitive landscape, the industry's growth prospects, and the overall economic outlook.

3. Select a valuation method. The best valuation method to use will depend on the specific circumstances of the business.

4. Calculate the business's value. This involves applying the selected valuation method to the financial information and industry analysis.

5. Review and finalize the valuation. Once the valuation has been calculated, it is important to review and finalize it with the client.

Business valuation is an important part of many business transactions. By understanding the business valuation process and working with a qualified professional, you can get an accurate valuation of your business.

Here are some additional tips for valuing a business:

* Use multiple valuation methods. This will help to ensure that the valuation is accurate and reliable.

* Consider the business's prospects. The valuation should take into account the business's potential for growth and earnings.

* Be realistic. The valuation should be realistic and based on sound assumptions.

* Be transparent. The valuation should be transparent and easy for the client to understand.

Various business valuation techniques might be applied, contingent on the unique conditions of the enterprise. The most popular techniques consist of:

Income approach

The income approach determines a company's value by looking at its potential for future profits. There are several distinct approaches to approaching revenue, such as:

* Discounted cash flow (DCF) analysis: This method values a business based on the present value of its future cash flows.

* Capitalization of earnings: This method values a business based on its current earnings and a capitalization rate.

* Earnings multiplier: This method values a business by multiplying its current earnings by a multiple.

*Asset approach

The asset approach values a business based on the net value of its assets. This method is often used for businesses with a lot of tangible assets, such as real estate and equipment.

Market approach

The market technique determines a company's value by looking at the prices at which similar companies have recently sold. This approach is frequently applied to companies that are comparable to other companies that have recently sold.

Which method to use

The best business valuation method to use will depend on the specific circumstances of the business. Some factors to consider include:

* The type of business
* The stage of the business's development
* The industry in which the business operates
* The availability of financial information
* The purpose of the valuation

If you are unsure which valuation method to use, it is important to consult with a qualified business valuation professional.

Here is a more detailed overview of each of the three main business valuation methods:

Income approach

The income approach is based on the principle that the value of a business is equal to the present value of its future cash flows. This approach is often used for businesses with a predictable earnings stream.

A variety of income approach techniques exist, such as capitalization of earnings, earnings multiplier, and discounted cash flow (DCF) analysis.

DCF analysis is the most sophisticated income approach method. It involves discounting future cash flows to the present value using a discount rate that reflects the riskiness of the business.

Capitalization of earnings is a simpler income approach method. It involves dividing the business's current earnings by a capitalization rate. The capitalization rate reflects the riskiness of the business and the expected growth rate of its earnings.

The earnings multiplier method is the simplest income approach method. It involves multiplying the business's current earnings by a multiple. The multiple reflects the riskiness of the business and the growth potential of its industry.

Asset approach

The asset approach values a business based on the net value of its assets. This approach is often used for businesses with a lot of tangible assets, such as real estate and equipment.

There are two main asset approach methods: the cost approach and the liquidation approach.

The cost approach values a business by reconstructing the cost of replacing its assets. The liquidation approach values a business based on the amount of money that could be raised if the business was liquidated and its assets were sold.

Market approach

The market technique determines a company's value by looking at the prices at which similar companies have recently sold. This strategy is frequently applied to companies that are comparable to other companies that have recently sold.

There are two main market approach methods: the comparable company analysis and the precedent transaction analysis.

Comparable company analysis involves comparing the subject company to similar companies that have recently sold. Precedent transaction analysis involves comparing the subject company to similar companies that have recently been involved in mergers and acquisitions.

Depending on the unique circumstances of the business, a variety of alternative business valuation techniques may be employed. The most common methods include the income approach, the asset approach, and the market approach. The best method to use will depend on the type of business, the stage of the business's development, the industry in which the business operates, the availability of financial information, and the purpose of the valuation.

How to value a business

Business valuation is the process of determining the economic value of a business. It is an important part of many business transactions, such as mergers and acquisitions, buyouts, and estate planning.

Businesses can be valued using a variety of techniques, but the most popular ones can be roughly categorized into three groups: market, asset, and income approaches.

Income approaches

Income approaches value a business based on its future earnings potential. The most common income approach method is discounted cash flow (DCF) analysis. DCF analysis involves discounting future cash flows to the present value using a discount rate that reflects the riskiness of the business.

Other income approach methods include capitalization of earnings and earnings multipliers. Capitalization of earnings involves dividing the business's current earnings by a capitalization rate. The capitalization rate reflects the riskiness of the business and the expected growth rate of its earnings. Earnings multipliers involve multiplying the business's current earnings by a multiple. The multiple reflects the riskiness of the business and the growth potential of its industry.

Asset approaches

Asset approaches value a business based on the net value of its assets. The two main asset approach methods are the cost approach and the liquidation approach.

The cost approach values a business by reconstructing the cost of replacing its assets. The liquidation approach values a business based on the amount of money that could be raised if the business was liquidated and its assets were sold.

Market approaches

Market approaches value a business based on the prices of comparable businesses that have recently sold. The two main market approach methods are comparable company analysis and precedent transaction analysis.

Comparable company analysis involves comparing the subject company to similar companies that have recently sold. Precedent transaction analysis involves comparing the subject company to similar companies that have recently been involved in mergers and acquisitions.

Choosing the right valuation approach

The best valuation approach to use will depend on the specific circumstances of the business. Some factors to consider include:

* The type of business
* The stage of the business's development
* The industry in which the business operates
* The availability of financial information
* The purpose of the valuation

If you are unsure which valuation approach to use, it is important to consult with a qualified business valuation professional.

Other factors to consider when valuing a business.

When evaluating a business, a variety of other aspects should be taken into account in addition to the valuation approach, such as:

* The business's management team
* The business's competitive landscape
* The business's intellectual property
* The business's customer base
* The business's financial condition

Here are some additional tips for valuing a business:

* Gather as much financial information as possible. This includes the business's income statement, balance sheet, and cash flow statement.

* Analyze the business's industry and market. This includes understanding the competitive landscape, the industry's growth prospects, and the overall economic outlook.

* Consider using multiple valuation methods. This will help to ensure that the valuation is accurate and reliable.

* Be realistic. The valuation should be realistic and based on sound assumptions.

* Be transparent. The valuation should be transparent and easy for the client to understand.

Chapter 9
Mergers and Acquisitions

What are mergers and acquisitions?

Mergers and acquisitions (M&A) are business transactions in which the ownership of companies, business organizations, or their operating units are transferred to or consolidated with another company or business organization. M&A transactions can be complex and involve a variety of legal, financial, and strategic considerations.

Types of mergers and acquisitions

There are two main types of mergers and acquisitions:

* Mergers: A merger is a transaction in which two or more companies combine to form a new company. The new company may be called either of the original companies, or it may be given a new name.

* Acquisitions: An acquisition is a transaction in which one company (the acquirer) purchases another company (the target). The acquirer may retain the target's name and branding, or it may integrate the target into its own operations.

*Why do companies engage in M&A transactions?

Companies engage in M&A transactions for a variety of reasons, including:

To grow their business: M&A transactions can help companies to grow their business quickly and efficiently. By acquiring another company, a company can gain access to new customers, markets, products, and technologies.

To expand into new markets: M&A transactions can help companies to expand into new markets that they would not be able to enter on their own. For example, a company that sells products in the United States may acquire a company that sells similar products in Europe to expand its reach into the European market.

* To increase productivity: By reducing overhead and simplifying processes, mergers, and acquisitions (M&A) can assist businesses in increasing productivity. For instance, a merger between two businesses in the same sector may be necessary to reduce overhead and increase profits.

* To get a competitive edge: Mergers and acquisitions (M&A) can provide businesses an edge over their competitors. To get rid of rivals, for instance, or to have access to their clientele or technology, a business can buy out its rival.

The M&A process

The M&A process typically involves the following steps:

1. Identification of targets: The acquirer identifies potential target companies. This may involve screening companies for financial performance, market share, and strategic fit.

2. Due diligence: Once a target company has been identified, the acquirer conducts due diligence to assess the target's financial condition, legal liabilities, and other risks.

3. Negotiation and structuring of the transaction: The acquirer and target negotiate the terms of the transaction, including the purchase price, payment terms, and other conditions.

4. Regulatory approval: In some cases, the transaction may require regulatory approval from government agencies.

5. Closing: Once the transaction has been approved by regulators and all other conditions have been met, the transaction closes and the acquirer takes ownership of the target.

Mergers and acquisitions can be a powerful tool for companies to grow their business, expand into new markets, improve their efficiency, and gain a competitive advantage. However, M&A transactions can be complex and involve a variety of risks. It is important for companies to carefully consider their strategic goals and objectives before engaging in any M&A transaction.

There are many different types of mergers and acquisitions (M&A) transactions, but some of the most common include:

Horizontal mergers: A horizontal merger is a transaction in which two or more companies that compete in the same industry merge. Horizontal mergers can be used to expand market share, reduce costs, and gain access to new technologies.

Vertical mergers: A vertical merger is a transaction in which two or more companies that operate at different levels of the same supply chain merge. Vertical mergers can be used to improve efficiency, reduce costs, and secure access to raw materials and supplies.

Conglomerate mergers: A conglomerate merger is a transaction in which two or more companies that operate in different industries merge. Conglomerate mergers can be used to diversify the acquirer's business, reduce risk, and gain access to new resources.

Market-extension mergers: A market-extension merger is a transaction in which two or more companies that sell the same products in different markets merge. Market-extension mergers can be used to expand into new markets and increase brand awareness.

Product-extension mergers: A product-extension merger is a transaction in which two or more companies that sell different but related products merge. Product-extension mergers can be used to expand the acquirer's product portfolio and offer customers a wider range of products.

Reverse mergers: A reverse merger is a transaction in which a private company merges with a publicly traded company. Reverse mergers can be used by private companies to go public without going through the traditional IPO process.

Acquihires: An acquihire is a transaction in which a company acquires another company primarily for the purpose of acquiring its talent. Acquihires are often used by technology companies to acquire startups with talented teams.

In addition to these basic types of mergers and acquisitions, there are many other variations, such as:

*Roll-up mergers: A roll-up merger is a transaction in which a company acquires a number of smaller companies in the same industry. Roll-up mergers are often used to consolidate an industry and create a larger, more dominant player.

* Spin-offs: A spin-off is a transaction in which a company divests a portion of its business by creating a new, independent company. Spin-offs are often used to focus on core businesses or to unlock value for shareholders.

*Track-and-tender mergers: A track-and-tender merger is a transaction in which an acquirer offers to purchase all or a portion of a target company's shares. Track-and-tender mergers are often used to avoid hostile takeovers.

The type of merger or acquisition that a company chooses will depend on its specific strategic goals and objectives. For example, a company that is looking to expand into a new market may choose to pursue a market-extension merger. A company that is looking to reduce costs may choose to pursue a vertical merger.

M&A transactions can be complex and involve a variety of legal, financial, and strategic considerations. It is important for companies to carefully consider their options and to consult with experienced professionals before engaging in any M&A transaction.

How to Structure and Execute a Successful Merger or Acquisition

Mergers and acquisitions (M&A) can be a powerful tool for companies to grow their business, expand into new markets, improve their efficiency, and gain a competitive advantage. However, M&A transactions can also be complex and risky. It is important for companies to carefully structure and execute M&A transactions to maximize their chances of success.

Here are some tips on how to structure and execute a successful merger or acquisition:

1. Have a clear strategic rationale. Why is the company engaging in the M&A transaction? What are the specific strategic goals and objectives of the transaction? It is important to have a clear understanding of the strategic rationale for the transaction before proceeding.

2. Identify the right target. The target company should be a good strategic fit for the acquirer. It should have a strong business model, a loyal customer base, and a talented team. The target company should also be financially sound and have a positive outlook for the future.

3. Conduct thorough due diligence. Due diligence is the process of investigating the target company to identify any potential risks or liabilities. It is important to conduct thorough due diligence on the target company's financial condition, legal liabilities, and other material matters.

4. Negotiate a fair price. The acquirer should negotiate a fair price for the target company. The price should be based on the target company's financial performance, market share, and other relevant factors.

5. Structure the transaction appropriately. The M&A transaction should be structured in a way that minimizes the acquirer's risk and maximizes its chances of success. This may involve using different types of equity and debt instruments, as well as earn-out provisions.

6. Obtain regulatory approval. In some cases, the M&A transaction may require regulatory approval from government agencies. It is important to obtain all necessary regulatory approvals before closing the transaction.

7. Integrate the target company effectively. Once the transaction has closed, the acquirer needs to integrate the target company into its own operations effectively. This may involve restructuring the target company, eliminating redundancies, and aligning the target company's culture with the acquirer's culture.

Here are some additional tips for increasing the chances of success of an M&A transaction:

* Communicate effectively with stakeholders. It is important to communicate effectively with all stakeholders about the M&A transaction, including employees, customers, and investors. This will help to minimize disruption and uncertainty.

* Manage change effectively. M&A transactions can lead to significant changes for employees, customers, and other stakeholders. It is important to manage change effectively to minimize disruption and maximize the chances of success.

* Be patient. M&A transactions can take time to close and integrate. It is important to be patient and to focus on the long-term strategic benefits of the transaction.

Different Types of Business Exit Strategies

A business exit strategy is a plan for the transition of business ownership either to another company or investors. Even if a business owner is enjoying good proceeds from his firm, there may come a time when he wants to leave and venture into something different.

There are several varieties of business exit strategies, and each has pros and cons of its own. An outline of a few of the most popular kinds of business exit plans is provided below:

* Selling the business to a third party. This is the most common type of business exit strategy. The business owner sells their business to another company, either a competitor, a strategic buyer, or a financial buyer.

* Going public. This involves selling shares of the business to the public through an initial public offering (IPO). This can be a good way to raise capital and to increase the value of the business. However, it is also a complex and time-consuming process.

* Management buyout (MBO). This involves the management team of the business buying the business from the current owner. This can be a

good way to ensure that the business continues to be run by a team that is familiar with and committed to the business.

* Employee stock ownership plan (ESOP). This involves selling shares of the business to the employees. This can be a good way to reward employees and to create a more motivated and engaged workforce.

* Liquidation. This involves selling off the assets of the business and distributing the proceeds to the owners. This is typically done when the business is no longer viable.

The best business exit strategy for a particular business will depend on several factors, including the size of the business, the industry in which the business operates, the financial condition of the business, and the goals of the business owner.

Here are some additional things to consider when choosing a business exit strategy:

* The value of the business. It is important to have a realistic understanding of the value of the business before choosing an exit strategy. This will help to ensure that the business owner gets a fair price for the business.

* The tax implications. Different business exit strategies have different tax implications. It is important to consult with a tax advisor to understand the tax implications of different exit strategies before deciding.

* The timeline. Different business exit strategies can take different amounts of time to complete. It is important to choose an exit strategy that fits the business owner's timeline.

How to Choose the Right Exit Strategy for Your Business

Choosing the right exit strategy for your business is an important decision that can have a significant impact on your financial future and the future of your business. Several aspects need to be taken into account while selecting an exit strategy, such as:

* Your goals and objectives. What do you want to achieve with your exit strategy? Do you want to maximize your financial return? Do you

want to ensure that your business continues to be run in a way that is consistent with your values?

* The performance and potential of your business. How well is your business performing? What is the potential for future growth?

* The valuation and deal structure. How much is your business worth? What kind of deal structure would be most beneficial for you?

* The timing and readiness of your exit. When are you ready to exit your business? Is your business ready to be sold or taken public?

Once you have considered these factors, you can begin to narrow down your choices and choose the exit strategy that is right for you.

Here are some of the most common business exit strategies:

* Selling the business to a third party. This is the most common type of business exit strategy. You can sell your business to a competitor, a strategic buyer, or a financial buyer.

* Going public. This involves selling shares of your business to the public through an initial public offering (IPO). Going public can be a good way to raise capital and to increase the value of your business. However, it is also a complex and time-consuming process.

* Management buyout (MBO). This involves the management team of your business buying the business from you. This can be a good way to ensure that the business continues to be run by a team that is familiar with and committed to the business.

* Employee stock ownership plan (ESOP). This involves selling shares of your business to your employees. This can be a good way to reward employees and to create a more motivated and engaged workforce.

* Liquidation. This involves selling off the assets of your business and distributing the proceeds to the owners. Liquidation is typically done when the business is no longer viable.

The best business exit strategy for you will depend on your individual circumstances and goals. It is important to consult with experienced professionals, such as a business broker, investment banker, or attorney, to help you choose the right exit strategy for your business.

Tips for Choosing the Right Exit Strategy

Here are some additional tips for choosing the right exit strategy for your business:

* Start planning early. It takes time to plan and execute a successful exit strategy. The sooner you start planning, the better prepared you will be.

* Get professional advice. A business broker, investment banker, or attorney can help you to assess your options, choose the right exit strategy, and negotiate a fair deal.

* Be flexible. The best exit strategy may change over time as your business and the market conditions change. Be prepared to adjust your plans as needed.

* Don't rush. It is important to take your time and choose the right exit strategy for your business. Don't feel pressured to sell your business if you are not ready.

Conclusion

The future of business and finance is rapidly changing, driven by technological advancements, globalization, and societal shifts. Here are some of the key trends that are shaping the future of business and finance:

Technological advancements are transforming the way businesses operate and compete. For example, artificial intelligence (AI) and machine learning are being used to automate tasks, improve decision-making, and create new products and services. Blockchain technology is being used to create more secure and efficient financial transactions. And the Internet of Things (IoT) is connecting billions of devices to the internet, generating vast amounts of data that can be used to improve business operations.

The world is becoming increasingly interconnected, and businesses are operating more globally than ever before. This is creating new opportunities for businesses to expand into new markets and reach new customers. However, it is also creating new challenges, such as complying with different regulations and managing complex supply chains.

Societal shifts, such as the rise of the millennial generation and the growing awareness of environmental and social issues, are also impacting the future of business and finance. Businesses are increasingly being held accountable for their social and environmental impact, and consumers are demanding more sustainable and ethical products and services.

Here are some specific examples of how the future of business and finance is being shaped by these trends:

* AI-powered businesses: AI is being used to create new businesses and to automate tasks and improve decision-making in existing businesses. For example, AI-powered chatbots are being used to provide customer service, and AI-powered algorithms are being used to make investment decisions.

* Blockchain-based finance: Blockchain technology is being used to create new financial products and services, such as decentralized exchanges and cryptocurrencies. Blockchain is also being used to improve the efficiency and security of traditional financial transactions.

* IoT-driven insights: Businesses are using data from IoT devices to improve their operations and to create new products and services. For example, manufacturers are using IoT data to optimize their production lines, and retailers are using IoT data to personalize the shopping experience for customers.

* Globalized supply chains: Businesses are increasingly sourcing goods and services from all over the world. This has led to more efficient and cost-effective supply chains, but it has also created new challenges, such as managing risk and ensuring compliance with different regulations.

* Sustainable businesses: Consumers are demanding more sustainable and ethical products and services. This is leading businesses to adopt more sustainable practices and to invest in renewable energy and other green technologies.

Advice for business owners and investors

Here is some advice for business owners and investors:

For business owners:

* Have a clear vision and mission for your business. What do you want to achieve? What are your core values? Having a clear vision and mission will help you to make informed decisions and to stay focused on your goals.

* Create a solid business plan. Your business plan should outline your business goals, strategies, and financial projections. A well-written business plan will help you to attract investors and to secure funding.

* Build a strong team. Surround yourself with talented and experienced people who share your vision. Your team will be essential to your success.

* Be customer focused. Always put your customers first. Listen to their feedback and use it to improve your products and services.

* Be innovative. Don't be afraid to try new things and to experiment. Innovation is essential for businesses to stay ahead of the competition.

* Be persistent. Entrepreneurship is not easy. There will be setbacks along the way. But if you are persistent and never give up on your dreams, you will eventually succeed.

For investors:

* Do your research. Before investing in any business, it is important to do your due diligence. This includes researching the business's financial performance, market position, and management team.

* Invest for the long term. Don't expect to get rich quick from investing. The best investments are those that you are willing to hold for the long term.

* Diversify your portfolio. Don't put all of your eggs in one basket. Spread your investments across different asset classes and industries to reduce your risk.

* Have a risk tolerance. Investing is inherently risky. It is important to understand your own risk tolerance and to invest accordingly.

* Don't panic sell. When the market takes a downturn, it can be tempting to panic sell your investments. However, this is often the worst thing you can do. Stay calm and stick to your investment plan.

Appendix

Financial Formulas and Calculators
Financial formulas and calculators are essential tools for businesses and individuals to make informed financial decisions. They can be used to calculate a variety of financial metrics, such as interest rates, present value, future value, and return on investment.

Here are some of the most common financial formulas and calculators:

Interest rate: The interest rate is the percentage charged on a loan or paid on an investment. It can be calculated using the following formula:

Interest rate = (Interest earned / Principal) * 100

Present value: The present value is the current value of a future sum of money, discounted at a given interest rate. It can be calculated using the following formula:

Present value = Future value / (1 + Interest rate) ^n

Future value: The future value is the value of a present sum of money at a future date, given a certain interest rate. It can be calculated using the following formula:

Future value = Present value (1 + Interest rate) ^n

Return on investment (ROI): ROI is a measure of the profitability of an investment. It is calculated by dividing the net profit of the investment by the total cost of the investment.

ROI = (Net profit / Total cost of investment) 100

Financial calculators can be used to simplify the calculation of these formulas. They are available in a variety of formats, including online calculators, mobile apps, and desktop software.

Here are some examples of how financial formulas and calculators can be used:

* A business owner can use a financial calculator to calculate the interest payments on a loan or the return on investment on a new product launch.

* An individual can use a financial calculator to calculate the monthly payments on a mortgage or the future value of their retirement savings.

* A financial advisor can use a financial calculator to create financial plans for their clients and to assess the risks of different investment options.

Financial formulas and calculators are powerful tools that can be used to make informed financial decisions. By understanding how to use these tools, businesses and individuals can improve their financial well-being.

Tips for Using Financial Formulas and Calculators

Here are some tips for using financial formulas and calculators:

* Understand the formula or calculator before using it. Make sure you understand what the formula or calculator is calculating and how to use it correctly.

* Be careful when entering data. Make sure you enter the data accurately to avoid errors in your calculations.

* Double-check your results. Once you have calculated your results, double-check them to make sure they are correct.

* Use financial formulas and calculators as a tool, not a replacement for expert advice. Financial formulas and calculators can be helpful tools, but they should not be used as a replacement for expert advice from a financial advisor.

Resources for Business Owners and Investors

A multitude of resources are at the disposal of entrepreneurs and investors to ensure their success. These resources can provide information on a variety of topics, such as starting and growing a business, investing in stocks and bonds, and managing personal finances.

Here are some of the most common resources for business owners and investors:

* Government agencies: The Small Business Administration (SBA) and the Securities and Exchange Commission (SEC) are two government agencies that provide a wealth of information for business owners and investors. The SBA offers a variety of programs and services to help small businesses start, grow, and succeed. The SEC provides information on investing in stocks and bonds, as well as on protecting investors from fraud.

* Trade associations: Trade associations are organizations that represent specific industries or sectors of the economy. They can provide information on industry trends, best practices, and networking opportunities. Some of the largest trade associations include the National Association of Manufacturers (NAM) and the Chamber of Commerce of the United States (USCC).

* Nonprofit organizations: Resources for investors and business entrepreneurs are offered by numerous nonprofit organizations. Some of these organizations focus on specific areas, such as small businesses or women-owned businesses. Others provide more general resources on topics such as investing and personal finance. Some of the most well-known nonprofit organizations that help business owners and investors include SCORE, the National Business Incubator Association (NBIA), and the Financial Planning Association (FPA).

* Educational institutions: Many colleges and universities offer business and finance programs. These programs can provide students with the knowledge and skills they need to start and grow a business or to invest successfully. Some educational institutions also offer non-credit courses and workshops on business and finance topics.

* Online resources: There are a number of online resources that provide information on business and finance. These resources can

include websites, blogs, and online communities. Some of the most popular online resources for business owners and investors include Entrepreneur.com, The Motley Fool, and Seeking Alpha.

Finding the Right Resources

With so many resources available, it can be difficult to know where to start. Here are a few tips for finding the right resources for your needs:

* Identify your needs. What are you trying to achieve? Are you looking for information on starting a business, investing in stocks and bonds, or managing your personal finances? Once you know what you are looking for, you can start to narrow down your search.

* Ask for recommendations. Talk to other business owners and investors, as well as to professionals such as accountants and lawyers. They may be able to recommend resources that have been helpful to them.

* Do your research. Once you have identified a few potential resources, take some time to research them. Read reviews, visit their websites, and contact them directly to ask questions. This will help you to determine which resources are the best fit for your needs.

Using Resources Effectively

Once you have found the right resources, it is important to use them effectively. Here are a few tips:

* Set aside time to learn. It takes time to learn about business and finance. Schedule time each week to read articles, watch videos, or take online courses.

* Be selective. There is a lot of information available on business and finance. Don't try to consume it all. Focus on the resources that are most relevant to your needs.

* Move forward. Read more than simply financial and business books. Use what you've learned. Make a budget, buy stocks and bonds, or launch a business.

Author: Ary S. Jr.

Milton Keynes UK
Ingram Content Group UK Ltd.
UKHW040707201123
432908UK00001B/166